Major John Scott

The conduct of his majesty's late ministers considered

as it affected the East-India Company and Mr. Hastings

Major John Scott

The conduct of his majesty's late ministers considered
as it affected the East-India Company and Mr. Hastings

ISBN/EAN: 9783743383784

Manufactured in Europe, USA, Canada, Australia, Japa

Cover: Foto ©Suzi / pixelio.de

Manufactured and distributed by brebook publishing software
(www.brebook.com)

Major John Scott

The conduct of his majesty's late ministers considered

THE

CONDUCT

OF

HIS MAJESTY'S

LATE MINISTERS

CONSIDERED,

AS IT AFFECTED

THE EAST-INDIA COMPANY

AND

MR. HASTINGS.

BY

MAJOR JOHN SCOTT.

LONDON:

Printed for J. DEBRETT, oppofite Burlington Houfe,
Piccadilly. M,DCC,LXXXIV.

TO THE

COURT OF PROPRIETORS

OF

EAST-INDIA STOCK,

WHO BY THEIR SPIRITED, AND
HONOURABLE SUPPORT OF THEIR SERVANT,

MR. HASTINGS,

AGAINST THE EFFORTS OF NUMEROUS,
AND POWERFUL ENEMIES,

HAVE PRESERVED AN EMPIRE TO GREAT BRITAIN,

BY CONTINUING HIM IN THE

GOVERNMENT OF INDIA,

UNTIL PEACE AND TRANQUILITY ARE COMPLETELY
RESTORED TO EVERY PART OF IT,

THE FOLLOWING SHEETS ARE DEDICATED WITH
THE SINCEREST RESPECT,

BY THEIR

MUCH OBLIGED AND

FAITHFUL HUMBLE SERVANT,

JOHN SCOTT.

Queen-Square,
10th Sept. 1784.

CONDUCT, &c.

THE Legiſlature has at length paſſed into a law, a bill for the better management of the affairs of the Eaſt-India Company. During its progreſs through the Houſe of Commons, the affairs of India have undergone a very full diſcuſſion, and, perhaps, this intricate ſubject is now much better underſtood by the public at large, than at any former period. The character and conduct of Mr. Haſtings has been a principal topic in every debate upon India affairs during the late ſeſſion. Lord North very juſtly obſerved, that Mr. Haſtings had been able to reſiſt every endeavour his Lordſhip made

to

to remove him : I may add, that his public character bore him up against an unjust, and abfurd refolution of the late Houfe of Commons. To fuppofe that money could have procured that honourable and effectual fupport which Mr. Haftings has received, even if he were rich enough, and mean enough to refort to bribery, is fo exceedingly ridiculous, that the men who infinuate the charge, do not, I am fure, ferioufly believe it. The fact is, that the people of England who fupported Mr. Pitt, this year, againft the madnefs and folly of the late Houfe of Commons, fupported Mr. Haftings in 1782 againft the fame body; with this difference however, that when the refolution for the recall of Mr. Haftings was carried, Lord Rockingham was the Minifter, and his party had great credit in the nation : of courfe to refift them was hazardous, though rendered in fome meafure lefs fo, from their own prefumption; but when they joined Lord North, they forfeited the confidence of the people, and confequently their attack upon Mr. Pitt, excited the popular indignation in a much greater degree than their injuftice to Mr. Haftings could do.

So

So many mifreprefentations have gone abroad, though their feafon for doing mifchief is at an end, that it will be but an act of juftice due to His Majefty's prefent Minifters, the Eaft-India Company, and Mr. Haftings, to prove, there has been no corrupt agreement between them; and that if they have appeared to act in concert, it was merel y becaufe the late Miniftry, at one and the fame time, attacked the Conftitution, the Company, and the well-earned fame of the prefent Governor General of Bengal.

Mr. Haftings certainly owes his fituation to the moft independent body of men in England, I mean the Proprietors of Eaft-India ftock, not, as I have heard it afferted, to a few men, who, for political purpofes, have purchafed ftock, and who compofe but one-fixteenth of the whole body, even if we fuppofe what is not true, that every gentleman who has ferved abroad and becomes a proprietor, does fo for political purpofes ; but from a very great majority of refpectable and independent men, who think they owe Mr. Haftings fupport in return for long, and faithful fervice, in difficult and arduous fituations.

That

That their confidence in him is ill placed, his enemies have long and vainly attempted to establish; that he merits their esteem, I shall endeavour to prove as I proceed.

Mr. Haftings has served the Company above four and thirty years. Immediately after the re-capture of Calcutta, he was confidentially employed by Lord Clive, and, I believe, the only person about him who did not acquire some fortune. He soon after succeeded Mr. Scrafton, as Resident at the Durbar of Meer Jaffier, the most advantageous office in the Company's service, where he remained until he became a member of the administration in 1761. In 1765, he quitted Bengal with a fortune so exceedingly moderate, that though he neither gambled, nor purchased estates, nor boroughs, nor was in any shape of an expensive turn, he was obliged to apply to the Court of Directors for permission to return to India at the end of three years. I appeal to gentlemen who have some knowledge of human nature, to determine whether it is probable that Mr. Haftings, who in the prime of life shewed so great a contempt for money, should go to such extraordinary lengths to obtain it

(as

(as his enemies have infinuated) at the age
of fifty-two. It will be in the recollection
of many, with what fcandalous and indecent
induftry that libel, entitled, The Eleventh Report of the Select Committee, was circulated;
that it was inclofed under a blank cover to
feveral members of the Houfe of Lords; and
that the charges contained in it were artfully
brought forward in fuch a manner, as to pre-
clude every poffibility of refutation, becaufe
they were declared " to be no charges, though
" they might hereafter furnifh matter for
" charge." I fhall juft add in this place, what
Mr. Burke declared to me in the month of
May, 1782, that there was a direct charge of
corruption againft Mr. Haftings. I was then,
and I am ftill, as ready to meet it as I was
to inveftigate the cafe of Almas Alhi Cawn,
or the Begums of Oude, from a conviction, that the more Mr. Haftings's conduct
is fcrutinized, the brighter it will appear. I
fhall not fay more on this fubject, than to defire that fome one perfon will produce the
charge of his corruption in office, and I pledge
myfelf to refute it. To the nonfenfe which
has been circulated fo inefficacioufly of large

fums

fums of money having been expended by me to preferve him in the government of Bengal, and to procure an influence in the prefent Parliament, I will merely obferve, that I am ready, publicly to produce an account of every fhilling that I have expended for Mr. Haftings or myfelf, fince my arrival in England; and the world will then be convinced, if farther conviction is neceffary, of the grofs falfehood of fuch affertions. *

In the progrefs of the India bill through the Houfe of Commons, fomething has been faid of the conduct of His Majefty's late Minifters towards Mr. Haftings. Lord North, with infinite wit and good humour, contrived to confound dates, circumftances, and proper names,

* An anonymous writer pledged himfelf to prove, that I had given one thoufand pounds in one year to the editor of a newfpaper; but when I publicly denied this fact, and called for the proofs, the writer was no more heard of. Infinuations of the fame kind have lately been thrown out in the Morning Herald. It fo happens, that the letters of Detector, a Citizen, and an Independent Proprietor, were originally publifhed in that paper; and if I paid more than the *market price* for their infertion I have done it ignorantly; however, I entertain no doubts upon the fubject: I dare fay I was fairly treated; and I do affure the editor of that paper, and the public, that I have paid at leaft four times as much to him as I have done to all the newfpapers in London put together.

in

in fuch a manner, as to amufe, if he did not inform the Houfe. Mr. Fox too, by talking in general terms of difobedience of orders, fervants being mafters, and many more to-pics drawn from the Reports of the Select Committee, drew their attention from the facts which I humbly attempted to eftab-lifh; but I deny that either Lord North, or Mr. Fox, or Mr. Francis, were able to dif-prove a fingle affertion that I have made. With refpect to the latter gentleman, his pre-dictions have fo uniformly been contradicted by the events, that I imagine the public will not place much confidence in his melancholy forebodings hereafter.

I have afferted that the war with the Ma-rattas, and every misfortune we have fuffered in India, originated in the American war, and in the meafures adopted in England. Mr. Fox made a fimilar obfervation in 1776. If the coalition had not taken place, I am fure he would prove it to be true. In the follow-ing detail of facts, fhould I miftate any cir-cumftances, or draw falfe conclufions from them, I fhall be expofed as I deferve.

Mr.

Mr. Haſtings ſucceeded to the government of Bengal in the month of April 1772, by the appointment of the Court of Directors. At this time the Company had reaſon to lament the very flattering account which Lord Clive had given them of the acquiſition of Bengal. His Lordſhip had ſtated the revenues too high, and the expences of government too low. By paying annually four hundred thouſand pounds to the State, dividing twelve per cent. upon the capital, and receiving bills from Bengal to a very large amount, in a ſeaſon of profound peace, they were reduced to the neceſſity of applying to Parliament for relief, and Lord North ſeized the opportunity of aſſuming the management of the Company's affairs. The injuſtice of this act is fully expoſed in that memorable proteſt, which the Dukes of Portland, and Richmond, Lords Rockingham, Fitzwilliam, &c. have tranſmitted to poſterity. The impolicy we have ſeverely felt. By the act of 1773, General Clavering, Colonel Monſon, and Mr. Francis, were appointed a majority of the Supreme Council of India. Mr. Haſtings continued Governor of Bengal, under the Directors ap-

appointment, from April 1772 to October 1774, a period of thirty months. In this time he had introduced order, regularity, and œconomy, into the government of Bengal, and he had provided funds for paying off the public debts which existed at the time of his arrival. The political measures of his government were, the withholding the tribute from the Mogul after he had withdrawn himself from our protection, and concluding a very advantageous treaty with Sujah Dowlah, by which a part of that treasure which had been so absurdly exported from Bengal was brought into it again. It was at this period that the Rohilla war was undertaken. Mr. Burke and Mr. Francis have not scrupled to attribute this war solely to Mr. Hastings; and they have asserted, that it was undertaken without a shadow of justice; that we exterminated a nation merely to acquire forty lacks of rupees. How gentlemen, who are at all acquainted with the history of India, can venture to hazard such assertions, is to me inconceivable; for the facts are directly the reverse, as a plain relation of them will prove.

In the year 1772, Sujah Dowlah and the Rohillas concluded a treaty, to which Sir Robert

C   Barker,

Barker, on the part of the Englifh, was the
guarantee. The article which gave rife to the
war was this: That if Sujah Dowlah and the
Englifh forces would affift the Rohillas, in ex-
pelling the Marattas from the Rohilcund, the
Rohillas engaged to pay forty lacks of rupees
to Sujah Dowlah. The engagement on our
part was faithfully performed: but on a fufpi-
cion that the Rohillas would evade theirs, Sir
Robert Barker, propofed to the Governor and
Council to put Sujah Dowlah in poffeffion of
their country on certain conditions, though the
Board declined the plan at that time. In three
feveral letters, dated in March and April 1773,
Sir Robert Barker, calls the Rohillas a faith-
lefs and treacherous race; fays, their non-com-
pliance with their engagements is notorious,
and the only way to compel them is to act upon
their interefts, or their fears. With thefe authentic documents, publifhed as they are in the
Fifth Report of the Secret Committee, how
any man can fay the Rohilla war was the war
of Mr. Haftings, or that we attacked the Rohillas without a pretence of quarrel, and yet
expect to preferve the fmalleft degree of credit
with impartial men, is beyond my comprehen-
fion.

fion. The Rohilla war was concluded on the 6th of October, 1774. General Clavering, Colonel Monfon, and Mr. Francis, arrived in Calcutta the 18th, and affumed the government the next day. To them were added Mr. Haftings and Mr. Barwell, becaufe, as Lord Lough-borough, and Lord North have informed us, it was thought neceffary that two gentlemen of local knowledge fhould be joined with thofe who went from England to a fervice fo perfectly new to them.

I do not mean to enter now into the particular fubjects of difpute between the majority and minority of the Supreme Council. The firft fhip that failed from Bengal carried a long letter written by Mr. Francis, and figned by the majority, in which every political act originating with Mr. Haftings was condemned: but before this letter arrived in England, the Directors had tranfmitted to Bengal their approbation of all Mr. Haftings's proceedings, the Rohilla war excepted; and I fcarcely think their fentiments on this fubject can be called a cenfure. They fay, " Notwithftanding the pecuniary advan-" tages which the Company have gained, we " are exceedingly concerned to find that our

" arms

" arms have been employed in the conqueſt of
" the Rohillas; though we muſt confeſs, the
" conduct of their chiefs, *in refuſing to fulfil*
" *their ſolemn ſtipulations, ſeems to have drawn*
" *upon them the calamities they have ſuffered.*"

Theſe were the ſentiments of the Court of
Directors upon the Rohilla war; and here the
ſubject would have dropped, if Lord North
had not determined to remove Mr. Haſtings,
and if a very improper degree of influence had
not been employed at the India Houſe to effect
his removal. The Rohilla war was again brought
forward, and moſt groſſly miſrepreſented. A
majority of one voice in the Court of Directors
determined, on the 8th of May, 1776, that
Mr. Haſtings ſhould be removed. Every poſ-
ſible exertion was made by Adminiſtration to
prevent the Proprietors from interfering with
effect in ſupport of Mr. Haſtings. Every clerk
in the public offices; every perſon poſſeſſing
ſtock, who could be influenced by Government,
was applied to. The intereſt of Lord North
and the Earl of Sandwich was very powerful
then in Leadenhall-ſtreet, and it was exerted
to the utmoſt.

I admire

I admire the ingenuity of the Ninth Report.
It contains, alfo, fome ftriking truths. To the
following I willingly affent, that after Lord
North's Regulating Bill paffed, " thofe who
" were engaged in contracts with the Treafu-
" ry, Admiralty, and Ordnance, together with
" the clerks in the public offices, found means
" of fecuring qualfications;" and it is fair to
conclude, that they voted with the Minifter:
but notwithftanding all the efforts of Adminiftration, and the induftry of their dependants,
Mr. Haftings obtained a complete triumph
through the honourable and virtuous affiftance
of the late Marquis of Rockingham, and every
independent man in England poffeffing India
ftock. At the time Lord North carried on the
American war by a majority in Parliament of
above four to one, he was defeated at the India
Houfe by a majority of 106 in 648, who bal-
lotted on the important queftion for the removal
of Mr. Haftings.

Lord North did not renew his endeavours
for his difmiffion. His Lordfhip knows the
fecret of the refignation I prefume. I have
related as far as Mr. Haftings is informed, in
a former Letter to Mr. Burke, and till the

Secret

Secret Committee of the Court of Directors, or Lord North, fhall comply with the earneft requeft of Mr. Haftings, and produce thofe powers which were faid to be ample and fufficient to authorize them in the acceptance of his refignation, the matter muft reft at it is.

From the moment intelligence arrived in England of the death of Sir John Clavering, every idea of removing Mr. Haftings was given up; and however earneftly Lord North might have laboured to effect it in 1776, he himfelf propofed in 1779, 80, and 81, that he fhould be continued the Governor General of Bengal by an act of the Legiflature; and certainly fupported him during thefe years, though with full knowledge of every ftep he was taking relative to the Maratta war, as well as of the motives by which he was actuated. I am not at all apprehenfive of being contradicted, when I fay, that His Majefty's Minifters and the Court of Directors approved of the Governor General's conduct, and that full and complete information was tranfmitted to them in the Minutes of Mr. Haftings and Mr. Francis, the former in defence of his meafures, the latter in reprobation of them.

When

When the firſt intelligence of the invaſion of the Carnatic was received in England, a Secret Committee was appointed to enquire into the cauſe of that invaſion ; and a few months prior to this, a Seleſt Committee had been inſtituted to conſider the ſtate of the judicature in Ben-gal. The objeſts of enquiry were ſo totally different, and the reports and proceedings of theſe Committees were ſo totally different, that I muſt deſire to conſider them ſeparately ; for though I entirely diſſent from the reſolutions brought forward by the Secret Committee, and am not afraid of aſſerting that ſeveral of them are unfounded, yet the Fifth and Sixth Reports are fairly and impartially drawn ; nor are any papers withheld, which tend to elucidate the ſubjeſt-matter of the Reports. But the Seleſt ✓ Committee, from the day they met in the ſe-cond ſeſſion of the laſt Parliament to the day of its diſſolution, appear to me to have had for their ſole objeſt the removal of Mr. Haſtings and all his Council ; and to effeſt this, they had ∧ recourſe to meaſures the moſt unfair and un-warrantable, as I have proved, and am ready at any time to prove again, to the ſatisfaſtion of any impartial man. Mr. Fox likes a ſyſ-tematic

tematic oppofition he fays ; and the Select Committee appears to have acted upon fyftem : the world will judge whether it was a juft one or not.

Lord North's adminiftration ended March 1782. It will be in the recollection of every gentleman, with what a degree of popularity the new Miniftry proceeded for fome time. Mr. Fox had a peace with America in his pocket, and Mr. Burke undertook to remedy all the diforders in our Eaftern government. Lord North and his friends appeared in force when Mr. Rigby's balances were under confideration, but on all other occafions there was a very thin attendance. In a few days after this great change, I heard Mr. Burke publicly declare, that Mr. Haftings and Mr. Macpherfon fhould be removed. The runners of Adminiftration without doors were bufily employed in circulating the groffeft and moft palpable falfehoods, in order to prejudice the public againft Mr. Haftings. The Secret Committee made four reports relative to the war in the Carnatic and the conduct of Sir Thomas Rumbold. In the Fifth and Sixth Reports they detailed the origin and progrefs of the firft and fecond Maratta

war

war fully and fairly; and they very flightly touched upon the political tranfactions in Bengal previous to the year 1775. In truth, this could form no part of their enquiry. It was alledged, that the Maratta war was the caufe of the invafion of the Carnatic; it was, therefore fair to trace it to its origin : but no event prior to it could at all affect the peace and tranquility of India. This will not now be difputed, though in the year 1782 it was fo much the fafhion to accufe Mr. Haftings of having forfeited the confidence of the natives of India.

On the 14th of April, 1782, the Chairman of the Secret Committee made a long fpeech, which was followed by various refolutions, forty-four in number, all tending to prove, that the policy of the Britifh Government in Bengal had been highly imprudent, and derogatory to the national honour, and that there had been much improper conduct at home. It was fomething fingular, that feveral of thefe refolutions, which were paffed in a very thin houfe, cenfured the Government of Bengal for withholding the tribute due to the Mogul, and the penfion of Nuzeph Cawn, as well as the fale of Corah and Allahabad. Thefe feveral mea-

fures

fures were adopted in the year 1773, had been communicated to the Directors, of courfe to His Majefty's Minifters, and had been highly approved of. If it was contrary to policy and good faith, as the feventh refolution afferts, to withhold the tribute from the Mogul, on his breaking off his connection with us, we ought in juftice to pay· up all arrears, or, at leaft, to remit the tribute to him in future; but the real fact is, that the Englifh affifted the Mogul when his fortunes were defperate, that they gave up two fertile provinces to him, and made him a remittance of twenty-fix lacks annually from Bengal, until, in fpite of all our remonftrances, he quitted our protection, and threw himfelf into the arms of the Marattas. This happened before Mr. Haftings returned to Bengal; and his conduct in a fituation which he did not create, but found exifting on his arrival, met with the warm approbation of his conftituents. The unhappy Mogul is fo far from attributing the misfortunes he has fuffered to Mr. Haftings, that he keeps up a conftant correfpondence with him, and depends upon the Governor General's good offices for affiftance againft the fucceffors of Nuzeph Cawn.

4

Expe-

Experience, also, has proved, that to purchase a passage for Colonel Pearce's detachment, was so far from being an extravagant and dishonourable act, as the thirty-ninth resolution asserts, that it was actually the means of breaking the grand confederacy, at the same time that it insured so great a reinforcement to Sir Eyre Coote. Equally unjust is the resolution which condemns the Supreme Council for attempting to procure military assistance from the Dutch, by the cession of Tinevelly. The Government of Madras had written to Bengal, representing their affairs to be irretrievable; it was then that Mr. Hastings proposed the Dutch treaty, leaving the Nabob and the Government of Madras to confirm it or not. A happy change in their situation enabled them to keep the field; they declined to accept the treaty; and the Supreme Council expressed their satisfaction in strong terms, declaring that they proposed it originally, upon an idea of its being better to sacrifice a part of their possessions, than to lose the whole. The first proceeding upon these extraordinary resolutions was, to pass another in a Committee of the whole House — that the Directors should remove those servants whom Parliament had

cen-

cenfured. This, however, was never reported.
Juft at this period fome confufed and imperfect
accounts of the infurrection at Benares were received in England. Thefe were greedily feized
by the Select Committee; and notice was given
to the Houfe of Commons on the 27th of May,
that a refolution for the removal of Mr. Haftings would be propofed on the following day.
When the refolution was read, I counted forty-
three members prefent, and Mr. Robinfon, of
Canterbury, very fhrewdly obferved, that it was
an extraordinary refolution to be propofed in
fuch a thin Houfe. Mr. Dundas, who propofed
it, expreffly ftated his reafons for fo doing; that
in his opinion Mr. Haftings had forfeited the
confidence of the native princes, and that therefore his removal was neceffary: but he fairly
declared, that he did not difpute the integrity,
or the abilities of the Governor General. Mr.
Fox on that day fpoke with great moderation.
Governor Johnftone, though differing in opinion with Mr. Dundas, declared very freely,
that if the Government of this country would
not give its confidence to Mr. Haftings, it
would be a right meafure to remove him: but
then it muft be done in a conftitutional manner,

by

by bill. Mr. Burke on this occafion held very ftrong language indeed. He declared, that any man, or body of men, who fhould dare to difobey a refolution of the Houfe of Commons, ought to be impeached. The refolution was carried, and tranfmitted to the India Houfe. Mr. Gregory and Sir Henry Fletcher filled the two chairs at the time : but the former gentleman having folemnly engaged not to carry into effect any refolution for the removal of Mr. Haftings, until it had been communicated to a General Court, we had time to look about us ; and on the 18th of June, a very full Court of Proprietors determined by a great majority, that to remove Mr. Haftings merely becaufe the Houfe of Commons had ordered it, would be wrong. Again they determined, that the Directors fhould not carry into effect any refolution which they might come to for the removal of Mr. Haftings, without previous communication to the General Court. No ftep whatever was taken in Parliament in confequence of this fpirited conduct of the Proprietors. Mr. Fox, indeed, did fay, that the fubject fhould be taken up in the next feffion : but a matter of more confequence to that gentleman and his party

than

than the falvation of India now happened,
The Marquis of Rockingham died on the 1ft
of July; and in the ftruggle for power at
home, Mr. Haftings was no longer remem-
bered. Mr. Fox's peace with America had
vanifhed, and he refigned, becaufe their in-
dependence was not inftantly acknowledged;
from which he predicted the happieft effects, had it been granted, though fubfequent
events have proved that he was much miftaken
in his conclufions. Thefe extraordinary proceedings in England had nearly deprived us of
India. Mr. Haftings, after having drawn off
Moodajee Boofla from the confederacy, having
fettled for the time with the Nizam, and fe-
cured a reinforcement of five regiments of fepoys to Sir Eyre Coote, was enabled, in the
month of October 1781, by having marched a
body of troops into Sindia's country, to conclude a feparate treaty with that chief. A total
ceffation of hoftilities with the Maratta ftate
immediately followed. A negociation was inftantly fet on foot for a general peace, and in
the month of May 1782, it was figned by Madajee Sindia and Mr. Anderfon, and tranfmitted
to Poonah to be ratified—but now we experienced

rienced the miserable confequence of the Government of India being counteracted by the Government at home. In the month of Auguft 1782, accounts were received at Poona, that the Miniftry had been changed, and that it was the determination of the new Miniftry to remove Mr. Haftings. The Marattas avowed their intention of waiting the arrival of his fucceffor before they ratified the treaty. Every month brought frefh intelligence that ferved to confirm them in this opinion. They knew perfectly well, that Mr. William Burke, who had been received with every mark of honour by the Rajah of Tanjore, was nearly connected with the gentleman of the fame name who filled a high office in England; and it is a fact of public notoriety, that fince the eftablifhment of the Supreme Council in 1774, the native Princes of India pay the utmoft attention to the political changes in Great Britain, fo far as they may be fuppofed to affect the politics of India. In the month of November 1782, accounts were received in India of the interference of the General Court in favour of Mr. Haftings, the death of the Marquis of Rockingham, and the refignation of Mr. Fox. Madajee Sindia con-
gratulated

gratulated Mr. Haftings on this happy change of affairs; and on the 20th of the next month the Maratta peace was formally ratified at Poona.

During the fummer of 1782, an enquiry into the conduct of Mr. Haftings was carried on at the India House. Mr. Gregory refigned the chair in Auguft, after having condemned in the moft pointed terms every act that originated with Mr. Haftings; and in order to weaken the Britifh Government as much as poffible at that critical moment, pofitive orders were fent for the immediate reftoration of Mr. Briftow and Mr. Fowke to Owde and Benares. In the month of October 1782, thirteen Directors paffed a refolution for the removal of Mr. Haftings. Whatever Lord Shelburne's fentiments might have been, he fupported this refolution, but it was refcinded by the determination of a moft refpectable Court of Proprietors; and if any man ftill believes the nonfenfe of the Proprietors being the fervants of the fervants in India, let him candidly attend to the following facts.

When Mr. Fox and Lord John Cavendifh refigned in July 1782, the former gentleman hinted in the Houfe, that amongft other caufes

of

of difcontent which induced him to give up, Lord Shelburne had fhewn a difpofition to pro- tect Eaft-India delinquents, and that he even expected him to bring in Lord North, but that the nation would not bear it. Perhaps his Lordfhip conceived, that if he could not venture to fupport Mr. Haftings, in confe- quence of the prejudice which then prevailed, it would be right to remove him, and he cer- tainly laboured to effect it. The gentlemen in the direction who voted for his removal, fupported it in the General Court. The Rock- ingham faction exerted themfelves on the fame account, yet fuch was the general conviction of the merits of Mr. Haftings, that all thefe in- terefts combined, could mufter but feventy-five votes upon a ballot, to oppofe to four hundred and twenty-eight. All the Proprietors who have ferved in India, refiding in Great Britain and Ireland, are one hundred and five, fo that if every man had attended and voted in favour of Mr. Haftings, ftill his majority of Englifh Proprietors whould have been very confidera- ble; but fo far from there being at that time a general agreement in his favour, I can point out feveral India gentlemen, added to General

E   Smith,

Smith, and Sir Henry Fletcher, who voted for his removal.

We were threatened with the vengeance of Parliament for this prudent exercife of our rights; but when it affembled in December, 1782, the expectation of peace prevented an immediate difcuffion of India affairs. The Select Committee was revived, and after the Chriftmafs recefs, a bill was promifed to be brought in : then followed the peace, and the overthrow of Lord Shelburne for having made it; for although Mr. Fox, in April, 1782, found the country " to be in a " much worfe fituation than even he had con- " ceived it to be before he came into office," and though " no peace, could then be a bad " one, we had experienced fo happy a change in our refources in nine months, that the terms agreed to by Lord Shelburne were fo dif- honourable, it was deemed better to coalefce with Lord North, than to fuffer his Lordfhip to remain in office. This bufinefs, however, was not immediately effected, and India was again left to itfelf. In the month of April, 1783, the coalition Miniftry affumed the government. The Select Committee had been diligently employed

ployed in inveſtigating the affairs of India, and,
on the 1ſt of April, they preſented a Report to
the Houſe, which appeared to ignorant men
to be intended merely for the purpoſe of keeping Mr. Sulivan and Sir William James out
of the direction, by exciting a clamour againſt
them juſt on the eve of our election, and before they could poſſibly have time to defend
themſelves. If this was the intention, it happily miſſed of its effect, Mr. Sulivan and Sir
William James, came in with a high hand, and
then Mr. Fox found out, that though this
matter was of conſequence, yet it was trifling
indeed compared to another which would ſoon
be before the Houſe. That all the world
knew there was a very important Report on the
point of being publiſhed, and that then ſome-
thing muſt be done in the affairs of India; and
then too he would conſider the Report which
affected Mr. Sulivan and Sir William James:
thus ended this trifling affair. Mr. Dundas's
bill was never read a ſecond time. At length
the famous Report alluded to by Mr. Fox appeared; it was intended to prove, that the
government of India was totally defective both
at home and abroad; and that horrible oppreſ-

ſions

fions had been committed in India, and winked at in England. Unfortunately, however, the bufinefs of Mr. Powell, and Mr. Bembridge, and other unlucky accidents, had fo foured the temper of the Houfe, that it was not thought quite prudent to attempt any thing that feffion againft Mr. Haftings, as his friends could oppofe to vague, and unfounded declamation, undoubted evidence of the moft folid and fubftantial fervices: the Maratta peace; the relief of Madras; and the improvement of the revenues of Bengal. This feffion of Parliament ended as the preceding one, by Mr. Fox pledging himfelf to do fomething effectual, as foon as the Houfe met after the recefs.

During the fummer of 1783, advices of great importance were received from India. The French had ftrained every nerve to diftrefs us; and in the midft of all the efforts of the Supreme Council to defend Madras, the Greyhound packet arrived with difpatches from the Court of Directors, tending to perfuade every man in Bengal that the removal of Mr. Haftings was near at hand. He had long borne up againft this fpecies of counteraction; but conceiving there was a determination to force

him

him from Bengal, and that without support
from home, he could not expect to conduct the
public business to advantage; he wrote in the
following terms to the Directors on the 21st of
March, 1783:

" It is now a complete period of eleven years
since I first received the nominal charge of
your affairs. In the course of it I have invari-
ably had to contend, not with ordinary difficulties, but such as most unnaturally arose from
the opposition of those very powers from which
I primarily derived my authority, and which
were required for the support of it. My exertions, though applied to an unvaried and consif-
tent line of action, have been occasional and de-
fultory: yet I please myself with the hope that,
in the annals of your dominion which shall be
written after the extinction of recent prejudices,
this term of its administration will appear not
the least conducive to the interest of the Company, nor the least reflective of the honour of
the British name; and allow me to suggest
the instructive reflection of what good might
have been done, and what evil prevented, had
due support been given to that administration
which

:which has performed such eminent and substan-
tial services without it.

" You, honourable Sirs, can atteſt the pa-
tience and temper with which I have ſubmitted
to all the indignities which have been heaped
upon me in this long ſervice. It was the duty
of fidelity which I eſſentially owed to it; it was
the return of gratitude which I owed, even
with the ſacrifice of life, had that been exacted,
to the Company, my original maſters, and moſt
indulgent patrons. To theſe principles have I
devoted every private feeling, and perſevered
in the violent maintenance of my office; becauſe I was conſcious that I poſſeſſed, in my integrity, and in the advantages of local knowledge, thoſe means of diſcharging the functions
of it with credit to myſelf, and with advantage
to my employers, which might be wanting in
more ſplendid talents; and becauſe I had always
a ground of hope that my long ſufferance would
diſarm the prejudices of my adverſaries, or the
rotation of time produce that concurrence, in
the criſis of your fortune with my own, which
might place me in the ſituation to which I aſ-
pired. In the mean time, there was nothing in
any actual ſtate of your affairs which could diſ-
courage

courage me from the profecution of this plan.
There was indeed an interval, and that of fome
duration, in which my authority was wholly
deftroyed; but another was fubftituted in its
place, and that, though irregular, was armed
with the public belief of an influence invifibly
upholding it, which gave it a vigour fcarce lefs
effectual than that of a conftitutional power.
Befides, your government had no external
dangers to agitate, and difcover the loofenefs
of its compofition.

" The cafe is now moft widely different. —
While your exiftence was threatened by wars
with the moft formidable powers of Europe,
added to your Indian enemies; and while you
confeffedly owed its prefervation to the feafona-
ble and vigorous exertions of this government,
you chofe that feafon to annihilate its conftitutional powers. You annihilated the influence
of its executive member—you proclaimed its
annihilation;—you virtually called on his af-
fociates to withdraw their fupport from him,
and they have withdrawn it. But you have
fubfiftuted no other inftrument of rule in his
ftead, unlefs you fuppofe that it may exift,
and can be effectually exercifed, in the body of

your Council at large; poffeffing no power of motion but an inert fubmiffion to the letter of your commands; which, however neceffary in the wife intention of the legiflature, have never yet been applied to the eftablifhment of any original plan or fyftem of meafures, and feldom felt but in inflances of perfonal favour or perfonal difpleafure.

" Under fuch a fituation, I feel myfelf impelled, by the fame fpirit which has hitherto animated me to retain my poft againft all the attempts made to extrude me from it, to adopt the contrary line. The feafon for contention is paft. The prefent ftate of affairs is not able to bear it. I am morally certain, that my fucceffor in this government, whoever he may be, will be allowed to poffefs and exercife the neceffary powers of his ftation, with the confidence and fupport of thofe, who, by their choice of him, will be interefted in his fuccefs. I am become a burden to the fervice; and would inftantly relieve it from the incumbrance, were I not apprehenfive of creating worfe confequences by my abrupt removal from it. Such an act would probably be confidered, by Mahdajee Sindia, as a defertion of him in the inftant of

his

his accomplifhment of the treaty, and defeat the purpofes of it, which remain yet to be effected by his agency. I am alfo perfuaded that it would be attended with the lofs of the commander in chief, in whofe prefence alone I look for the reftoration of peace to the Carnatic, which he, perhaps, would think too hazardous an undertaking with no other fupport than that of a broken government. I have now no wifh remaining, but to fee the clofe of this calamitous fcene, and for that I hope a few months will be fufficient. My fervices may afterwards be fafely withdrawn; but will ftill be due, in my conception of what I owe to my firft conftituents, until they can be regularly fupplied by thofe of my appointed fucceffor, or until his fucceffion fhall have been made known, and the interval but fhort for his arrival.

"It therefore remains to perform the duty which I had affigned to myfelf as the final purpofe of this letter; to declare, as I now moft formally do, that it is my defire that you will be pleafed to obtain the early nomination of a perfon to fuccceed me in the government of Fort William; to declare that it is my intention to refign your fervice as foon as I can do it with-

out

out prejudice to your affairs, after the allow-
ance of a competent time for your choice of a
perſon to ſucceed me; and to declare, that if,
in the intermediate time, you ſhall proceed to
order the reſtoration of Rajah Cheyt Sing to
the Zemindary, from which, by the powers I
legally poſſeſſed, and conceive myſelf legally
bound to aſſert, againſt any ſubſequent authority to the contrary derived from the ſame common ſource, he was diſpoſſeſſed for crimes of the
greateſt enormity, and your Council ſhall re-
ſolve to execute the order; I will inſtantly give
up my ſtation and the ſervice."

However deſirous the friends of Mr. Haftings might have been to retain him in the
government of Bengal, here was an earneſt requeſt from himſelf to be relieved. No ſtep
was taken either by the Directors or his Ma-
jeſty's Miniſters in conſequence of it. The
letter was received in September laſt, and the
following month the Court of Proprietors
voted him their thanks for his ſervices; to
which they added, a requeſt that he would not
reſign until the complete reſtoration of peace in
India, and the arrangements in conſequence of
it had taken place.

This

This was the precise situation of affairs when the late House of Commons met on the 14th of November. When the resolution passed in a thin House in May 1782 for the recal of Mr. Hastings, we were at war with the Marattas, with Hyder Ally, the French, and the Dutch. A strange idea prevailed, that Mr. Hastings had forfeited the confidence of the native Princes, and that his removal was necessary, as a step preparatory to peace. Subsequent events had proved the fallacy of this opinion. Mr. Hastings made the Maratta peace; he relieved the Carnatic; Hyder was dead; and a peace had been concluded in Europe; Bengal was in a perfect state of tranquillity; and the revenues were annually improving.

On the first day of the session, the 11th of November, Mr. Fox informed the House, that he would open the heads of a bill for the government of India on the following Tuesday. Every possible exertion was made to insure success to his plan; a very artful pamphlet had been published, and generally distributed previous to the meeting of Parliament, in which the grossest misrepresentation were inserted, in order to prejudice the public against the East-India Company and

Mr.

Mr. Haſtings*. The newſpapers were well ſupplied with paragraphs tending to the ſame end. The Select Committee, a very few days after they aſſembled, publiſhed their Eleventh Report without an Appendix. This was inſtantly re-printed by Mr. Debrett, who during the ſummer had printed the Ninth Report alſo; and leſt the world ſhould want an inducement to read them, they were advertiſed as containing an account of the conduct of Mr. Haſtings, and of money acknowledged to have been received by him. Theſe Reports were ſent to the preſent Lord Chancellor, amongſt other Peers, under a blank cover. Is it therefore extraordinary, that feeling an honeſt indignation at a proceeding ſo ſcandalous, his Lord-

---

* A conſiderable part of this pamphlet is very much in the ſtyle of Mr. Fox's ſpeech when he opened his plan. Speaking of the Select Committee, the writer ſays, " This Committee " is compoſed of gentlemen of the moſt unſullied probity and " firſt-rate talents, whoſe knowledge of the ſubject cannot be " queſtioned, and whoſe induſtry and perſeverance are only to " be equalled by their candour and fairneſs. To diſtinguiſh " individuals without naming the whole, would be invidious. " The proceedings of this highly reſpectable Committee have " been always open and public. The teſtimony of witneſſes " has been taken in the moſt ſolemn manner."

Theſe are a few of the compliments paid to the Select Committee; and the author then gives up ſome extracts from the Ninth Report, which he ſtyles an " invaluable document."

ſhip

fhip fhould have declared, that to fuch Reports
" he would pay as much attention as to the
" Adventures of Robinfon Crufoe."

On the 18th of November, Mr. Fox, in a
very long fpeech, opened his plan. Inftead of attributing the temporary diftrefs of the Eaft-India
Company to their true caufes, the American
war, and the pernicious interference of Minifters,
which no man formerly reprobated in harfher
terms than himfelf, he now declared, that our
misfortunes were owing to the mifmanagement
of Mr. Haftings in India, and to the fupport
which he met with from his agents and dependents at home. In the courfe of his fpeech,
he went through all the unfounded charges
that have been infinuated in the Reports of the
Select Committee; and after defcribing Mr.
Haftings as a corrupt, ambitious, and unprin-
cipled Governor, he moved for leave to bring
in a bill not to remove, not to punifh the Governor, but totally to annihilate the privileges
of his conftituents, for which he affigned two
curious reafons; the one, that the Proprietors
were become the fervants, of the fervants in India; the other, that they were unfit, by their
conftitution, for the management of an empire.

pire. The firſt is one amongſt many fanciful ideas which are to be found in the Ninth Report; but to prove the truth of it, nothing like the ſhadow of an argument has ever yet been offered. To mention the conqueſts acquired during the war by the Eaſt-India Company, and the honourable manner in which they have terminated it, would be the completeſt anſwer that could poſſibly be given to the ſecond aſſertion. During the many diſcuſſions that this famous bill received in the Houſe of Commons, Mr. Fox and his friends varied their ground very often. They explained away, in ſome meaſure, what had been ſaid of the bankruptcy of the Company. It had been ſtated in all the newſpapers that Mr. Fox declared, we had but three millions two hundred thouſand pounds to pay a debt of above eleven millions. This ſunk the ſtock near fifteen per cent. in one day.

It is impoſſible not to take notice of a very curious circumſtance which paſſed on the day the bill was read a ſecond time: Mr. Fox diſputed the items of the Company's account, article by article, in the moſt ingenious and entertaining ſpeech I ever heard. The Company

had

had stated the amount of their cash, bonds, and notes, to be above six hundred thousand pounds, then lying in their Treasury in Leadenhall Street.

After a few items more, there was the following " Silver remaining in the Treasury for " exportation — one thousand and ninety " pounds." There cannot be a greater proof of the advantage acquired by this nation, from the acquisition of Bengal, than the following : — That from the commencement of the present century to the year 1764, the average of silver exported was near 400,000l. each year; but from 1764 to the present time, it is a mere trifle. A considerable quantity of specie has been brought into the kingdom from India since 1764. But how did Mr. Fox turn this? He appeared totally to forget the former sum of cash in the Treasury, six hundred thousand pounds, and observed, " The next item was, silver remaining in the " Treasury, 1090l. The only notice which he " meant to take of this article was, to declare " his astonishment, or, rather indeed, not his " astonishment, but to point it out as a fact " which proved his statement of their finances

" to be right. After enumerating their millions
" afloat, their millions in the warehouſes, they
" came to the calculation of their ſpecie, and it
" amounted to the ſum of 1090l. This re-
" minded him of an article in one of our Great
" Bard's beſt plays, where, ſpeaking of one of
" his beſt characters, it is ſaid, ' So much for
" ſack — ſo much for ſugar — ſo much for
" burnt hock — ſo much for this, and ſo much
" for that; but for the ſolid, the ſubſtantial,
" the ſtaff of life — bread, one halfpenny.' So
" it was with this flouriſhing Company: they
" had millions of goods, of bonds, of debts;
" but of ſilver they had one ſolitary thouſand
" pounds."

This remark was received with the ſtrongeſt
ſigns of approbation in the Houſe: it was repeated in every newſpaper the following day;
and I am ſure the firſt impreſſion the Public
received was, that the Company's Treaſury
contained but a ſolitary thouſand pounds on the
28th of November laſt.

The preamble of Mr. Fox's bill runs thus:
" Whereas diſorders of an alarming nature and
" magnitude have long prevailed, and do ſtill
" continue and *increaſe*, in the management of
" the

" the territorial poffeffions, the revenues, and
" commerce of this kingdom in the Eaft In-
" dies, by means whereof the. profperity of
" the natives hath been greatly diminifhed, and
" the valuable interefts of this nation, in the
" faid territorial revenues, &c. have been ma-
" terially impaired, *and would fall into utter
" ruin,* if an immediate and fitting remedy
" were not provided." The arguments of Mr.
Fox and his friends intirely coincided with the
fpirit of this preamble *. Mr. Haftings and
Sir Eyre Coote were declared not to wifh for
peace. †They perfecuted the excellent Lord
Macartney, becaufe he was defirous of accom-
plifhing it. God only knew whether that noble Lord had not fhared the fate of Lord Pigot.
It was doubtful whether India could be faved at
all, or peace reftored; but it was only to be

---

* Mr. Fox. " The feeds ofwar were already fown in India;
and a note left by Sir Eyre Coote, a man who deferved every
poffible praife, independent of his gallant actions, afforded
alarming proofs of it."

† Mr. Fox. " Did the Houfe know of the difputes in our
Prefidencies? That Lord Macartney, that great and exalted
man, the only man who paid obedience to his conftituents,
was at this inftant perhaps removed, confined, perhaps come
to the fate of Lord Pigot?" — Vide Debrett's Debates for
November, 1783, pages 160 and 172.

effected,

effected, if poffible to be effected, by an immediate change of fyftem; and therefore the bill ought to pafs without delay. This was the language of its fupporters; and when, happily for the nation, it was thrown out, they prefented an addrefs to the Throne, in which they fay, " That the diforders prevailing in the Eaft In-" dies call aloud for *inftant* reformation."

On the fame day that Mr. Fox moved for leave to bring in his bill, a packet failed from Bengal, conveying to us the fulleft proofs that the ftate of India was at that time the very reverfe of what it had been reprefented, and that the only difficulties the Government of Bengal laboured under were occafioned by the abfurd conduct of His Majefty's Minifters at home. We learnt that on the 18th of November the Carnatic had been nearly evacuated; that the conditions of the peace with the Marattas had been faithfully executed on both fides; that we had concluded an eventual treaty with them, in order to compel Tippoo Sultaun to accept of reafonable terms; and that the only object of concluding that treaty was to accelerate the peace with him. That our army had been confiderably reduced, and that farther reductions

ductions

du&ions were determined upon as foon as our
foreign detachments fhould reach Bengal. That
the Supreme Council, though highly difapprov-
ing the conduct of Lord Macartney, had determined to await the decifion of the Court of Directors. This was the actual fituation of affairs in
India at the moment the late Miniftry propofed
fo violent a meafure. Subfequent advices have
been ftill more favourable; and there is not a
man of common underftanding in England who
muft not fee that the preamble of the India
bill was founded in mifinformation, or that His
Majefty's late Minifters were determined to ex-
aggerate the diftreffes they had themfelves crea-
ted, in order to feized the patronage and property
of the Eaft-India Company for their own fecu-
rity. That we have participated in the calamities which have nearly overwhelmed this country is certain — That the prodigious efforts made
by France to difpoffefs us of India, could not
have been fo fuccefsfully repelled without great
and enormous expences, no man will doubt —
That in fo long a war, fome individuals muft
have acquired money is true; but what proportion do the fortunes lately gained in India bear
to the acquifitions of individuals in England

during

during the unfortunate American war? Yet it
was the fashion, laft winter, for Mr. Fox and
his friends to hurl the thunder of their eloquence at the devoted Eaft-India Company. —
If any impartial man examines the funds of the
Company, I am fure he will form a patriotic
wifh, that this nation may have as fair a profpect
of being extricated out of all her difficulties as
the Eaft-India Company has at the prefent
moment.

The India bill paffed the Houfe of Commons
by a prodigious majority. — Mr. Macdonald
very fhrewdly obferved, that to carry this enormous defign through, three different grounds
had been laid on three different days. On the
firft day, it was the fuppofed mifconduct of Mr.
Haftings: on the fecond, the fuppofed bankruptcy of the Company; and on the third, a
radical defect in the prefent fyftem.

Lord John Cavendifh afferted, "that the bill
" was fuch a meafure as the fituation of affairs
" required. Nobody but a child, or a trifler,
" would think of continuing the prefent confti-
" tution of the India Company." I have too
good an opinion of the integrity and honour of
Lord John Cavendifh, to fuppofe he would
have

have made fuch a declaration, unlefs he had
been convinced at the time of the truth of it.
The fame obfervation I apply to the other
gentlemen who fupported it; but it is now
proved, beyond contradiction, that the Houfe
and the Public were egregioufly mifled, fince
every fhip that has arrived from India during
the fummer, has brought full and complete
proof, that our affairs, fo far from being in
danger of falling into " *utter ruin,*" are in a
ftate of profperity, which far exceeds the hopes
of the moft fanguine of our well wifhers.

In the Houfe of Lords, the fame arguments
that had been fo fuccefsfully urged in the
Houfe of Commons were repeated, but with
very different effect. The Company were pa-
tiently heard by their Counfel, and they proved
to the fatisfaction of every impartial man, that
the preamble of the bill was totally unfounded.
The fupport the bill met with was exceedingly
feeble; but the fpeeches of the Duke of Richmond, Lords Thurlow, Camden, Walfingham,
and other noble Lords, in reprobation of fuch
a fyftem as the bill went to eftablifh, effectually convinced the Houfe and the Public,
that they had been hitherto grofsly deceived.

The

The Lord Chancellor in particular, moſt happily expoſed the abſurdity and the iniquity of puniſhing the Company, for the alledged miſconduct of Mr. Haſtings, and fairly declared, that it would be ſcandalous in the higheſt degree to permit Mr. Haſtings to eſcape if he was guilty, or to brand him with the name of delinquent if innocent. If Mr. Haſtings, or his friends in his abſence, had ever deprecated the vengeance of his opponents, *if they had bargained for his ſafety by continuing to ſtand neuter at this critical moment*, there might have been ſome ground to ſuppoſe, that his conduct would not bear a ſcrutiny; but this was ſo far from being the caſe, that Mr. Haſtings has ſaid, " if I have violated the national faith, no " puniſhment ſhort of death can atone for the " injury which the intereſt and credit of the " State has ſuſtained*." This is the language

---

* Many are the honourable teſtimonies of eſteem and regard which Mr. Haſtings has received from gentlemen who are utter ſtrangers to him, and totally unconnected with the politics of India. The following much-admired paſſages are extracted from the letters of Mr. Day to Mr. Burke, publiſhed under the ſignature of Marius.

I muſt confeſs it ſtrikes me with no little idea " of the in- " conſtancy of human greatneſs, and the ſtupendous revolu- " tions

guage of Mr. Haſtings in India; the language
of his friends in England has been the ſame;
Mr. Fox, if he really thought Mr. Haſtings
" an uſurper and a ſcourge to mankind, a
" cruel

" tions that have happened in our age of wonders," when I
ſee a ſet of men, who have juſt loſt Thirteen Provinces, fitting
in judgement upon, and diſpoſſeſſing thoſe, who have added
to the Britiſh empire " 281,412 ſquare miles, which form a
territory larger than any European dominion, Ruſſia and
Turkey excepted." Whatever may be now advanced by inte-
tereſt or malevolence about the crimes or incapacity of the
Company's ſervants, is amply confuted by the unexaggerated
detail of events. What ſtronger evidence can be given of the
ſolid baſis upon which any human power is founded, than its
capacity to reſiſt and triumph over the mightieſt attacks? This
even, excluſively, is the boaſt of the Eaſt-India Company.
With every diſadvantage of difficulty and diſtance, it has
prevailed not only over the feeble oppoſition of Aſiatic Princes, but over all the efforts of one of the moſt politic and war-
like nations in the univerſe. Could this have been effected
without a ſpirit both of counſel and of enterprize? No;
whatever may be the repreſentations of parliamentary orators,
the world at large will refute the wild and chimerical accuſa-
tion. Whatever may be the demerits of the Company, whatever the catalogue of its crimes, the comparative ſeries of its
Miniſters may certainly vie with that of any modern government in Europe. It has undoubtedly produced warriors of
intrepid minds, and heroes of immortal fame; chiefs that
have dared in their employers' and country's cauſe, all that
men can dare, that have executed every thing which the
preſent colleagues of Mr. Burke *have failed to do.* Even
now, " on evil days, though fallen, and evil tongues," it
can boaſt of charaɛters that would do honour to any nation;
the foremoſt of whom is that very culprit that ſeems ſingly
like an electric rod upon a noble edifice, to have protected
the

" cruel and a defperate man, whom from his
" heart and foul he detefted and execrated*,"
has acted, as a public man, moft unwarranta-
bly. The honour of the nation is concerned
not to permit an ufurper to efcape with impu-
nity, and fupported by fo powerful a majority
as Mr. Fox lately was, if he could have fubftantiated a fingle charge againft Mr. Haftings,
he could have removed him inftantly by bilL
To fay that Mr. Haftings had an influence in
Parliament to bear him up againft the eloquence
and power of Mr. Fox, if he had been " a
" notorious delinquent," would be to impofe
upon mankind. During the madnefs of the
Rockingham Adminiftration, when the Houfe
of Commons paffed a refolution, " that it
" was the duty of the Directors to recal Mr.
" Haftings;" no gentleman offered to divide
the Houfe, and the obfervations made upon

the building beneath, while he attracts the fury of the tem-
peft upon himfelf. Yet even he, "fcathed" as he may appear, with all the lightnings of parliamentary vengeance,
nor afks the mercy, nor deprecates the rage of his accufers:
he is ready to leave the throne of half the Eaft, in order to
meet their impeachments; he bids them take his life, if any
thing worthy of death fhall be found in his conduct; nor
dare his moft inveterate enemies accept the offer.

* Mr. Fox's fpeech, Dec. 17, 1783.—Debrett's Debates,
Vol. XII,

the occasion, were first by Governor Johnstone,
that if Ministers were determined to remove
him, they did not go the right way to do it;
and next by the worthy member for Canterbury, who said, that the House was rather
thin (forty-three members present) consider-
ing the great importance of the resolution.
What accession of interest or influence had Mr.
Hastings acquired in twenty months, that
should support him in the same House of Commons, against such an host of able and powerful opponents? The fact is, he was defended
by the people of England, who had sense
enough to see through the arts that were prac-
tised to depreciate the character of the man who
has preserved every thing in Asia, while in other
quarters of the globe we have lost every thing;
and who asked no other favour from the late
Ministers, than to be brought before some tribunal, where he could be permitted to defend
himself. During the progress of the bill
through the House of Commons, many efforts
were made to effect this, and particularly by
Governor Johnstone, who declared, repeatedly,
that the foundation of the bill being built on
the pretended misconduct of Mr. Hastings, it

H   was

was as unjuft as it was abfurd, not to bring forward fpecific charges againft that gentleman. All his efforts were vain, for Mr. Fox continued to declare, that the merits or demerits of Mr. Haftings were not then a fubject of confideration, but when the fame line was taken in the Houfe of Lords by one noble Peer; the prefent Lord Chancellor declared, as in truth and juftice he was bound to do, that it would be impoffible to difcufs the bill without entering fully into the merit or mifconduct of Mr. Haftings; the confequence was, that Lord Walfingham's reply to the fpeeches of Lords Carlifle, and Sandwich, was a moft complete refutation of every thing that had been faid relative to Benares, Oud, and a variety of fubjects which had been partially inveftigated in the Reports of the Select Committee. Not an argument ufed by the noble Lords who oppofed the bill, was anfwered, or even an attempt made to reply to their objections.

All that had been faid of the bankruptcy of the Company, of the mifconduct of Mr. Haftings, of the cabals and intrigues between the fervants in India and their dependents in England, moft happily miffed its effect. The bill

was

was defervedly loft, and every day, every hour
brings conviction to the mind of every man, that
the affertions made by thofe who fupported the
bill had no foundation in fact, that they were
artfully calculated to catch the prejudices of the
moment, with the hope that a meafure, big with
fuch important confequences to our happy conftitution, would have paffed, before the Public
were fenfible of its pernicious effects.

When Mr. Fox propofed the bill, we laboured
under every poffible difadvantage. Our Chairman, who was bound to be our protector, was
one of the feven Commiffioners, and was to
have rifen upon the ruin of the Company.—If
he thought the bill a good one, he was right to
fupport it; but from the moment he took that
line, he fhould have difqualified; it was not,
however, till the fecond reading that he quitted
the direction. It was with difficulty we could
procure the infertion of any articles in the daily
papers (one excepted) which tended to difprove
the flagrant falfehoods that were hourly circulating. But when the bill was before the Houfe
of Peers, our reprefentations began to have fome
effect; and I defire the moft prejudiced party
man in England to contradict me if he can,

when

when I affert, that every letter received from India in the courfe of the prefent year, has fully juftified the ftatements we laid before the Public.

The bill was thrown out by the Lords on the 17th of December, and the change of Miniftry followed. In the firft tumult that fucceeded this event, we now and then heard of Mr. Haftings, and of India. The former was ftated to be an ufurper, but upon what ground I know not. If the gentlemen who report Mr. Fox's fpeeches are accurate, he has decidedly affirmed, " that India would be loft without inftant reformation; Thirty millions of innocent people were groaning under every fpecies of oppreffion, and fecret influence had deftroyed the ftrongeft Adminiftration this country had ever been bleffed with." Thefe fubjects, however, were very foon abandoned for others of infinitely greater importance to the late Adminiftration. But at length the Parliament was diffolved, without any plan for the government of India being adopted: and here again I muft obferve, how unfortunate His Majefty's late Minifters were in their predictions laft year. It was declared, that without the inftant adoption of fome plan, India would be loft; a bill muft pafs before February, and perhaps all the expedition

they

they could ufe would not fave that country. Have
not events, univerfally known, now moft completely proved, how fallacious and unfounded
thefe apprehenfions were. Peace is completely
reftored, retrenchments have been made, and
the revenues greatly improved; where then is
" that utter ruin," in which, according to the
preamble, we were to be involved, " if an im-
" mediate and fitting remedy was not pro-
" vided."

While the bill, that has lately paffed for the
better government of India, was under difcuffion, much was faid of the conduct of Mr.
Haftings, and the influence he had acquired in
this kingdom; his difobedience of orders, and
contempt of fuperior authority, were frequently
mentioned.

With refpect to Mr. Haftings's influence in
England, whatever may be the degree of it, I
can fafely affert, that it has been fairly and ho-
nourably acquired, and that he may glory in it;
that there never was a man in a public ftation,
fo totally unconnected with the parties which
divide this kingdom as Mr. Haftings is, that
he has neither courted Mr. Fox, nor Mr. Pitt,
and all he has ever required has been, fairly and

openly

openly to be supported if he deserves support, or
to be recalled if thought unworthy of confidence;
he has never sought to preserve his station by
cabal and intrigue, and has ever held that bold,
decided language in Bengal, which every man of
spirit must esteem him for.   That Mr. Hastings
has, by corruption, by bribery, or by any means
whatever that would degrade the character of
a gentleman, obtained influence of any kind in
England, I solemnly deny;—not a shadow of a
proof has been offered to convince the world,
that he has resorted to such base means of support.   Two or three very good things, indeed,
have been said, as to the number of Indians
now in Parliament, but I have proved, that
there were precisely the same number in the last;
the only difference is, that the balance was then
in favour of Mr. Fox, and now it is on the side
of Mr. Pitt.   It has also been wittily observed,
that the Treasury Bench was under the India
Bench in the last session, but here, again, I cannot help recollecting, that I have seen General
Smith, Captain Sir Henry Fletcher, and Mr.
Jacob Wilkinson upon that Bench, and I cannot
help thinking, that Mr. George Vansittart, Colonel Call, and myself, were as well intitled

to all thofe feats, as the gentlemen who formerly occupied them.

Mr. Haftings has been accufed, in general terms, of difobedience of orders, and Mr. Fox attributed the wars in India to his difregard of the inftructions he received from home; — but from this charge Mr. Dundas moft completely defended him, by proving, that whether the Maratta war was politic or not, fo far as Mr. Haftings was concerned in it, he was fully jufti-fied by the exprefs orders of the Court of Di-rectors, — and he might have gone farther, for thofe orders had the exprefs fanction of his Majefty's Minifters; though one fet of gentle-men appear now to be totally ignorant, not only of this circumftance, but of the very im-portant intelligence tranfmitted to Bengal by Mr. Elliot, and inferted in the Appendix to the Sixth Report of the Secret Committee. — I have already detailed the events which gave rife to the Rohilla war in 1773, and it was commenced, and ended in fix months. Thefe are the only hoftilities in which we have borne a part in Bengal during the laft twenty years,— but a ftranger, who was to read the late parlia-mentary debates, would really fuppofe we had

been

been engaged in perpetual war in Bengal ;—
though in truth, at no period of the modern
hiftory of Indoftan, has that country enjoyed
fo long a peace, as fince the Englifh acquired
the government.

It was afferted *, that Mr. Haftings difobeyed
a peremptory order for the reftoration of Cheyt
Sing, but no orders of this kind ever were
fent ; and abfurd, and mad I might almoft fay,
as the conduct of the late Minifters, with refpect
to India, has been, I can fcarcely conceive it
ever was in contemplation to reftore him. —
The whole of the proceeding relative to Cheyt
Sing was ftrictly confonant to the conftitution
of the government under which he lived. —He
has been ranked here amongft the native princes
of India, 'but his family owed its confequence
entirely to the Englifh. His father, Bulwant
Sing, was originally a petty zemindar in the
diftrict of Juanpore, and paid about four thoufand rupees a year to the government : he then
became collector or farmer of a diftrict under
his fovereign Sujah Dowlah, and at length was
appointed the collector of Benares. — In this

* Mr. Fox's fpeech, 16th of July.

fituation

fituation we found him when Sujah Dowlah was
marching to invade Bengal. — We protected
him againft the vengeance of his Sovereign in
1764, and he was confirmed in the zemindary,
by the treaty of Allahabad, in 1765. — From
that time to the day the fovereignty of Benares
was transferred to the Company, Sujah Dowlah
required military affiftance from Bulwant Sing
and his fon Cheyt Sing, whenever his forces
took the field, and he received it *. — We
made a fimilar demand when the war broke out
with France, and Cheyt Sing promifed to comply with it.—That he evaded his promife I attribute entirely to the diffentions in our councils
and his expectation of a change in the government.

In this bufinefs of Cheyt Sing there is a
circumftance that, I confefs, furprifes me exceedingly, which is this : The gentlemen who
have argued upon it feem totally to forget that
the demand of money had been made three fuc-
ceffive years previous to the infurrection, and
compliance enforced by military execution. —

* For proof of this, fee the evidence given by Colonel
Harper to the Select Committee in 1781, long before the
infurrection at Benares.

I   A very

A very particular detail of each year's proceedings was tranfmitted to England in triplicate. Did his Majefty's late Minifters, or did one gentleman in the direction ever give an opinion that Mr. Haftings and his council had violated the national faith by demanding, on the part of the Company, military affiftance from their vaffal Cheyt Sing? — Certainly they did not, nor was fuch an idea ever entertained till it became the fashion to decry the character of Mr. Haftings. — Yet Mr. Gregory and Sir Henry Fletcher were in the direction at the period when the demands were made, and the confequences communicated. Lord North was the Minifter, too, at the time. — Shall thefe gentlemen be excufed for their conduct, and shall Mr. Haftings now be calumniated? He and his Council acted right. —As guardians of the Britifh intereft in India, they demanded what, in their idea, was the Company's right; but if there were men in office in England of a different opinion, as it feems there were by their fubfequent conduct, they are criminal in not protefting againft a meafure which was deemed a violation of the national faith.

The

The other inftances of difobedience of orders which have been quoted were the not fending Mr. Briftow to Oud and Mr. Fowke to Benares. — Is there a man of common fenfe in England who can now entertain a doubt upon this fubject ? Thefe gentlemen were made the inftruments of a party, and Mr. Pitt may as fairly be accufed of criminality for not keeping Mr. Sheridan or Mr. Richard Burke in the Treafury, as Mr. Haftings has been for declining to fend Mr. Briftow and Mr. Fowke to Benares and Oud, at the moment when every newfpaper in Indoftan contained accounts that thefe appointments were made in confequence of a determination at home to difmifs Mr. Haftings, and that his difmiffion might hourly be expected. — I confefs the idea is fo repugnant to common fenfe, of continuing a man at the head of an empire, and refufing him at the fame time the privilege of appointing thofe who are to fill the firft political ftations in it, that I am aftonifhed how a gentleman of Mr. Fox's talents can take that ground.— Mr. Haftings ftated it fairly in Bengal. — The bill lately paffed has ftated it fairly too.— Obedience to orders is pofitively injoined, — but

in.

in inftances where orders are difobeyed, the
proof of the necefſity for fuch difobedience
muſt be full, or punifhment will follow. —
Such was the language of Mr. Haftings. —
He never expected a repetition of the orders
relative to Mr. Briftow and Mr. Fowke. —
He affigned his reafons for acting as he had
done, and, if they were not fatisfactory, he
expected difiniſſion himſelf.

Critical, indeed, was our fituation when this
bufineſs was agitated. The Carnatic had juft
been invaded: The peace with the Marattas
was not concluded; a French armament was on
its way to India ; and Sir Eyre Coote, with a
large reinforcement, was on the point of proceeding to Madras. At this moment, Mr. Francis propofed that Mr. Briftow fhould be fent to
Oud, agreeable to the order of the Directors.
I defy any man living to controvert the reafons
affigned by Mr. Haftings, for refufing to carry
the order then into execution. Sir Eyre Coote
equally felt the impolicy of the meafure, but
he had committed himſelf, and therefore agreed
to it, wifhing Mr. Haftings to adopt fome
plan that fhould tend to prevent any bad effects from the appointment. Our fituation
growing

growing more defperate in India, Mr. Haftings recalled both Mr. Briftow and Mr. Fowke.
It was hard to bring him to a perfonal conteft
with two junior fervants of the Company.
Surely in the fituations they filled, it was fufficient to fay, that having been fent there by his
opponents, when party was at the higheft in
Bengal, they could not be fuppofed to be his
particular choice, though he wifhed to do them
no injury, and was defirous of employing them
in any other line.—The intelligence of the removal of thefe gentlemen, arrived in England at
the very time * when we were reafonably alarm-
ed by the prodigious efforts which France was
making to difpoffefs us of India. Lord North
was then the Minifter, and Mr. Sulivan the
Chairman of the Directors. They had too much
good fenfe to think of weakening the Government of Bengal, at that critical moment, by
agitating a perfonal queftion. But though the
ftate of India became ftill more defperate,
when the Rockingham Adminiftration came
in, yet the Select Committee, and a bare
majority of the Directors, cordially co-ope-
rated in bringing forward every meafure that
could diminifh the credit of the Government

* December, 1781.

I

of

of Bengal, or weaken its exertions for the public fervice. While Mr. Burke did me the honour to examine me on the bufinefs of Mr. Briftow and Mr. Fowke, Mr. Gregory and Sir Henry Fletcher were ordering their reftoration, and cenfuring the conduct of Mr. Haftings in the harfheft language. I think Mr. Fox once obferved, during the late war, that Lord North and Lord Sandwich could not do the bufinefs of France more effectually than they did, had they been bribed to the fervice. I am fure I can apply this remark to the conduct of the Rockingham Adminiftration, refpecting India in 1782.

It has been infinuated, that Mr. Haftings's motive for difobeying the orders of the Court of Directors, was in order to ftrengthen his Parliamentary-intereft at home, by providing for Gentlemen who had great and powerful connections here ; but furely there never was a more unfounded charge than this is. Mr. Briftow's connections in England were very powerful. He had two near relations in Parliament, Lord Weftcote and the late General Frafer. He was patronized by Lord North's Adminiftration. Mr. Middleton, on the other hand, was fcarcely known in England except to Mr. Gregory, who

who had taken so hostile a part against the Governor-General: Mr. Bristow came out at a time when his Lordship was desirous of supporting the Governor-General. If Mr. Hastings had studied to strengthen his own interest at home, he could not have done it more effectually than by patronizing Mr. Bristow.

Mr. Fowke was nearly related to Gentlemen with whom Mr. Hastings had passed the early part of his life. It was neither for his interest, nor his ease to remove him, nor was it probable that he would be in a situation to want the service of Mr. Markham's friends in England: That Gentleman had been his private secretary; he thought him the best qualified for the residency of Benares, at the very critical minute in which he appointed him: but surely any candid man, who considers the case, will be convinced that Mr. Hastings neither acted from motives of enmity to Mr. Fowke, nor in order to insure the good offices of the Archbishop of York in Great Britain. I do not know a single instance in which Mr. Hastings has attended either to the mean gratification of personal resentment, or to the establishment of a powerful interest in England, by the disposal of patronage

aage in India. If the conduct and characters
of the civil, and military fervants who have been
peculiarly employed by him, are fcrutinized, it
will be found that no man in a public ftation,
has been more fortunate in diftinguifhing and
employing in the public fervice men of honour
and abilities than Mr. Haftings; and that he has
never been at the pains to enquire whether their
connections in England were powerful or net *.
It is the peculiar fate of Mr. Haftings to be accufed by one fet of men, of wafting the public
money for private purpofes, and by another, of
being totally inattentive to the recommendations
of thofe who have the power of fupporting him
at home.

In the courfe of the proceedings in Parliament
on India affairs, the terms ufurper and delinquent have been applied to Mr. Haftings; and
Mr.

* To prove this I could bring many inftances. Mr. Shore
is one of the number; that Gentleman is called by Mr. Burke
a " Creature of the Governor-General," becaufe he was the
leading member in the management of the Revenue of Bengal,
during the abfence of Mr. David Anderfon. But the truth is,
that Mr. Shore had always lived in focial intimacy with Mr.
Francis, and was patronized by Mr. Haftings, from the high
opinion he entertained of his abilities in the Revenue Line,
without the fmalleft regard to his political opinions, or connections.

Mr. Dundas in particular, has been called upon to proceed againft him as a delinquent. I could wifh the public would attend to a curious fact, which that gentleman ftated in the moft direct and manly terms. He faid, there were gentlemen prefent, who knew that he had been applied to formerly, to proceed againft Mr. Haftings as a delinquent, but that he had peremtorily refufed to do fo; and for the beft reafon in the world, becaufe he did not believe Mr. Haftings was a delinquent, nor had he ever thought him one: That he propofed his removal, from an opinion that he had forfeited the confidence of the native Princes of India, and that it was neceffary, as a ftep preparatory to peace.—I can aver, that this is no new idea of Mr. Dundas; for, upon a former occafion, while the Marratta peace was depending, he declared his intention of removing Mr. Haftings by bill; but he exprefsly ftated, that it was upon the idea of its being a meafure of expediency, and not from an opinion of his delinquency. It is very neceffary this circumftance, fhould be attended to, becaufe a party in this country have wifhed to fpeak of the two Committees, as if they perfectly coincided in their

K   fentiments

sentiments of Mr. Haftings, yet nothing can be more diffimilar than their opinions, and their conduct. Every thing that Mr. Dundas thought Mr. Haftings could not do, he has actually accomplished, in fpite of the obftructions which were thrown in his way, by the miferable politics of this country; fo that every caufe of objection to Mr. Haftings is removed, and it is no difcredit to Mr. Dundas, to acknowledge that he was miftaken, or, that though his reports are fair and impartial, the conclufions he drew from them are contradicted by fubfequent events.

But the Reports of the Select Committee go upon very different ground; they certainly were intended to fix a very great degree of criminality upon Mr. Haftings. The effence of all thefe Reports is contained in Mr. Burke's printed fpeech of the 2d of December laft, in which that gentleman fairly and fully appealed to the tribunal of the Public, and before the fame refpectable tribunal I alfo appeared.—To mere declamation I cannot reply; but when pofitive affertions are made, they are capable of proof, or contradiction. I have proved, by facts which are not to be controverted, that Mr. Burke

has

has miſtated a great variety of ſubjects; amongſt the reſt may be mentioned "The Rohilla War;" "the Maratta War;" "Mr. Haſtings's Treatment of the Mogul," "the Vizier, "the Begums of Oud;" "Diſobedience of Orders:" Management of the Revenues; the Opium Contract; and "the Bullock Contract:" I have fully replied to, and I have fully refuted all theſe charges:, though it is a peculiar hardſhip attending Mr. Haſtings, that while the moſt powerful, and the ableſt men in this kingdom have been diligently employed in effecting his ruin, they have declared, that his conduct was not the object of enquiry; and even the Ninth Report, which, from the firſt page of it to the laſt, (I mean Mr. Debrett's Report) is the moſt intemperate libel againſt him that ever was publiſhed, has the following paſſage:—"The Reports of your "Committee are *no charges*, though they may "poſſibly furniſh matter for charge."

Since I am upon the ſubject of the Reports of the Select Committee, I cannot avoid taking notice of a circumſtance which I have publicly mentioned—that the evidence of Lieutenant-Colonel Robert Stuart, a gentleman who had been examined two days by the Select Commit-

tee,

tee, was completely fuppreffed. The Tenth Report was made in order to prove that Mr. Haftings had been guilty of a breach of public faith, in withdrawing the Company's guarantee from the Begums of Oud, by which means, the Vizier had re-affumed their Jaghires, and acquired poffeffion of his father's treafures. Upon the fubject of the Begums, I had the honour to be examined, and my evidence is entered in the Appendix to the Tenth Report. Lieutenant-colonel Harper (who quitted India in 1773) was alfo examined, and his evidence is entered. Colonel Stuart was alfo examined, who had then juft arrived in England, (February, 1783) and appeared peculiarly calculated to give material information, by having commanded a detachment in the Vizier's country ; but not the fmalleft reference is made to his evidence in the Report, *and it is not entered in the Appendix.* In fhort, it remains at this moment amongft the mafs of minutes taken by the Select Committee.

Colonel Stuart was examined on the 19th and 20th of February, 1783 ; and in anfwer to the queftions put to him, he faid, that he had ferved in India for many years, that he had commanded a detachment for ten months in Rohilcund, that

he

he never heard complaints of exactions by fepoys or officers in our fervice, from the Zemindars or inhabitants; that he left Oud in June, 1781, the cultivation of the country was impaired from the time he firft knew it ; — that the Nabob Vizier had complained to Mr. Middleton, that his refources were much decreafed, and that he wifhed to ftrike off the heavy burthen of the Jag-hirdars ; — that he thinks Mr. Middleton men-tioned this to him in the latter end of 1780; — that it was currently reported and believed, that ever fince a few months after the late Vizier's death (in 1775), both the Begums, and the Nabob's Uncles were all combined in a fcheme againft the Britifh intereft :—he heard that fome correfpondence, explanatory of that inimical difpofition, had fallen into our hands: — he thinks (in 1777) Zabita Cawn, the fon of Nad-jub Ul Dowlah, fent an ambaffador to the Vizier with a paper, faid to be the original of a confe-deracy entered into by the different Powers of India, to act in concert with the French, to ex-pel the Britifh from India ; and that the Begums and Uncles, his relations, were faid to be con-cerned in it : — that this circumftance was told him by the ambaffador of Zabita Cawn ; that he

does

does not know of any act of hostility committed ; but Nudjeff Cawn declared his intention of entering the Vizier's country in a hostile manner, and as he commanded the Western Province, he took every precaution to frustrate his intentions : that Nuzeph Cawn never did enter the country, in an hostile manner, as he knows of ;—that he does not know the military force of the Begums, but thinks they could not have raised two regiments of sepoys :—that the Vizier attributed the decline of his country, to the specie being drawn from it ; that the cause of that drain was, *the subsidies paid to the Company, and the public debts due by the late Vizier to the Company ; and that there was a constant flow of treasure from Oud to Bengal* : — that the Vizier did complain of the distress brought upon him by the number of troops kept in his country ; and that, in consequence, they were recalled from Rohilcund and Futtygur ; and several English gentlemen were also recalled :—*That he first heard of the indisposition of the Begums to our Government, a very few months after the death of Sujah Dowlab* (in 1775) : — That he does not know of any Treaty entered into by the English to protect the Begums in possession of their property : — that

when

when the ambaffador of Zabita Cawn made the communication to him, he paffed through his camp, and paid him a complimentary vifit :— that he did not communicate this intelligence to Mr. Haftings, as the ambaffador told him it had been communicated to the Refident at Lucknow, which he believed, or he fhould certainly himfelf have fent intelligence of it to the Council General.

These are fome of the material parts of Colonel Stuart's evidence; and furely it applies infinitely more to the fubject matter of the Tenth Report, than any part of my evidence, or that of Colonel Harper's, but *it was wholly fuppreffed.* Shall I not then rejoice that a tribunal is eftablifhed, which will fuperfede this mode of inveftigation ?— The injuftice of the proceeding can only be equalled by its abfurdity, unlefs the fact were really as it is ftated to be in the Ninth Report:—" That the Committee makes no " charge."— But is that the cafe ? I appeal to the good fenfe of every man in England to determine that it is not.— A committee is appointed; with power to fend for papers, to examine evidences, and to draw up Reports.— Under thefe powers they examine feveral gentlemen as to a

particular

particular fubject : one of them, an officer of
high rank and character, is afked a number of
queftions relative to the ftate of Oude, and the
conduct of the Begums : his replies tend very
fully to confirm what Mr. Haftings has afferted,
and to juftify his conduct towards thofe ladies :
but the whole is fuppreffed. From no part of
the Tenth Report, could the world fuppofe that
there is fuch a man, as Lieutenant-colonel Robert Stuart, in exiftence. But as the Reports are
no charges, this is deemed of fmall confequence ;
and whenever a charge is made, fay the Repor-
ters, " It will be at the difcretion of the party
" accufed, to call for, and for the difcretion of
" the Houfe of Commons to inftitute fuch pro-
" ceedings, as may tend finally to condemn or
" acquit." 9th Report, page 33.—I hope every
man of honour will attend to the manner in
which this doctrine is applied.

A Report thus imperfect, thus partial, is fent
into the world. The friends of Mr. Haftings
are not to reply to it, becaufe " the Committee
" make no charge," and his hour of trial is not
come : yet every thing that Mr. Fox has faid of
Mr. Haftings's conduct to the Vizier and the
Begums, he actually drew from this partial

and

and imperfect Report. — How often was it obferved, while his India bill was depending. " If
" any man thinks that the moft flagrant enor-
" mities have not been committed in India, let
" him look to the Reports upon your table."
Such was the language in both Houfes, till the
Lord Chancellor, with a dignity and fpirit be-
coming his high character, declared, " That to
" fuch Reports he would pay as much attention
" as to the Hiftory of Robinfon Crufoe."

There is not a fyllable in the Reports,
there was not a fentence uttered while Mr.
Fox's bill was before the Houfe of Commons, that had a reference to depending
events, which has not been contradicted by
the lateft advices from India. How much has
been faid and written of the miferable ftate of
Oud, of the oppreffion the Vizier laboured under
from Mr. Haftings, and of his being com-
pelled by the Governor General to plunder
the Begums. The balance due from the Vizier
to the Company, was pronounced to be a defperate debt, and the unfortunate Directors were
accufed of audacity for prefuming to include it
in their accounts — We now find that the
Vizier, his Minifters, and the principal people

L   of

of his court, place the moſt implicit reliance on the juſtice and good faith of Mr. Haſtings— That above eight lacks of rupees of his balance were actually paid in February laſt, and un-doubted ſecurity given for the diſcharge of the whole debt. It is proved, that at the repeated and earneſt requeſt of the Vizier, Mr. Haſtings conſented to his reſumption of the Begum's Jaghires, and that upon his requeſt they have ſince been reſtored to him. We now find that every rupee of the Vizier's debt will be realiz-ed, and without our having recourſe to thoſe dreadful means for its recovery which a warm imagination painted in ſuch glowing colours, and deſcribed as the common mode by which debts were recovered in India.

It was aſſerted that in the Maratta peace, we had laid the foundation of a new war — but will any man now regard ſuch an aſſertion? Much was ſaid of Mr. Haſtings' permitting the Vizier to plunder Fyzoolla Cawn, and it was made the ſubject of a Report, but the engagement with him has been faithfully obſerved, and he has lately applied to Mr. Haſtings to aſſiſt him in the ſecuring the ſucceſſion of his Jag-hire to his eldeſt ſon —. In no inſtance does it

it

it appear, that * we are execrated in India, or
that our government is deemed a curfe by the
natives — Men who know as little of India, as
I do of the Orkneys, have repeatedly declaimed
upon this fruitful fubject, while the popular
prejudices were ftrong; but who is there of
any information, who does not know, that from
the death of Aurungzebe, to the total deftruction
of the Mogul empire by the invafion of Nadir
Shah, India was a fcene of blood and rapine —
To that period indeed, a period of near fifty
years, many of the defcriptions that I have heard
would in part apply; but are the countries
under the immediate management of the Englifh
deferted or laid wafte? Will any man who tra-
vels through Bengal and Bahar, ferioufly fay
with the compiler of the Ninth Report, that
the inhabitants are reduced to the loweft ftate
of depreffion and mifery—Yet by fuch flowery
declamation were the People of England for a
time mifled — In all the Reports of the Select
Committee, in all the fpeeches upon the management of Indian revenue, not a line or a word

---

* See Parliamentary Debates while the rejected India bill
was depending.

has

has appeared in honour of a man who deferves
fo much of his country as the late Mr. Cleveland — That gentleman had the glory of fub-
duing by mildnefs and humanity a barbarous
and favage race of men — the inhabitants of
the weftern mountains of Bengal — Thefe
people were not be conquered by force of arms,
and they committed continual depredations,
plundering the villages on the plains, murder-
ing the inhabitants, attacking boats upon the
Ganges, and cutting off paffengers from time
to time. — During the country government
many attempts were made, if not for their extir-
pation, at leaft for their fubjection, but they
are now become obedient and ufeful fubjects—
They cultivate their lands, fubfift upon its produce, and yield a revenue to the Government,.
Mr. Cleveland fell a facrifice to his unremitting
attention to the office he held, the collector of
the revenues of Boglipoor; and Mr. Haftings
has paid the only tribute he could pay to fo
valuable a man, by ordering a monument to be
erected to his memory, in a country where
while living he was fo much efteemed, and
where his death is lamented by Europeans and
natives of every rank.

Even

Even the merit of Mr. Cleveland could not secure us from the severity of Mr. Burke's remarks; but if he really learnt his leſſon from Mr. Francis *, and ſpoke from his works as from a brief, I am ſure that gentleman muſt have told him, that great as Mr. Cleveland's merits were, he was not the only gentleman in Bengal whoſe abilities and integrity would do honour to any ſervice in the world. — Could Mr. Francis inform Mr. Burke that " Our conqueſt " there (in Bengal) is as crude as it was the " firſt day," — Impoſſible, I think; and yet Mr. Burke avows not only that he himſelf, but every member of the late Houſe of Commons who learnt any thing good, learnt it from Mr. Francis.

Much has been ſaid of the influence Mr. Haſtings poſſeſſes in England; and that though not perſonally preſent†, he appeared this year in the Houſe of Commons by his repreſenta-

---

* This man, whoſe deep reach of thought, whoſe large legiſlative conceptions, and whoſe grand plans of policy, make the moſt ſhining parts of our Report, from whence we have all learned our leſſons, if we have learned any good ones; this man, from whoſe materials thoſe gentlemen who have leaſt acknowledged it, have yet ſpoken as from a brief, &c.

† Mr. Francis's ſpeech of the 2d of July.

tives.

tives. An expreſſion of this kind can only be calculated " *ad captandum vulgus*," and even there will miſs of its effect; for of the whole number of India gentlemen who fit in Parliament, there is not one (myſelf excepted) in the ſucceſs of whoſe election Mr. Haſtings was in the ſmalleſt degree intereſted. He has not even contributed a ſhilling towards the expence of the Weſtminſter election. There was a time when ſpeeches, " full of pointed ſatire," had a very great effect; but Mr. Haſtings's character is fortunately now ſo far fixed with the Public, that they will require poſitive charges to be brought and fully proved, before they condemn a man who has preſerved an empire to Great Britain. Hitherto every charge againſt him has been found to originate in ignorance, or prejudice.

I have been much ſurpriſed to hear gentlemen, confeſſedly of great abilities, expreſs a wiſh that we had never acquired territorial poſſeſſions in India, and to hear them aſſert, that we are execrated by the natives; that our Government has been a grievance and a curſe to them. It is a ſatisfaction to reflect, that we never attempted acts of hoſtility until we were

wantonly

wantonly attacked. In our progrefs to empire have we been guilty of thofe horrid cruelties which are a difgrace to other European nations, who have acquired kingdoms in India, and America? Mr. Burke feems to acquit us here; but he fays, " It is our protection that deftroys " India." I never yet met with a native of Bengal or Bahar in the middling or lower clafs of men, who did not declare that he preferred being under the Englifh Government to any other. The fentiment, I believe, is univerfal, except amongft that order of men with whofe advantages, ftations, and views, we muft necef-farily have interfered; I mean the great Maho-metan officers; and except we were to expel all the Muffulmen from Indoftan, of what ad-vantage would it be to the Aborigines of the country, that all Europeans were driven out of it? I know not by what right Tamerlane ac-quired or the defcendants of Tamerlane pof-feffed the empire, but by conqueft: they, re-tained it for many centuries. The Mogul em-pire was at length deftroyed by Nadir Shah's invafion. From that period, till the tyrant, Surajah Dowlah, attacked the Britifh factory in Calcutta, we are told by an impartial hifto-rian,

rian *, that " the country was torn to pieces
" by civil wars, and groaned under every spe-
" cies of domestic confusion. Villainy was
" practiced in every form; all law and religion
" were trodden under foot; the bands of private
" friendship and connections, as well as of so-
" ciety and government, were broken, and
" every individual, as if amidst a forest of wild
" beasts, could rely upon nothing but the
" strength of his own arms."

Will any man who reads this description,
and knows any thing of the state of Bengal under the English, seriously assert, that our Government has been a curse, and that we were execrated throughout the country? The East-
India Company have obtained no advantages by
the acquisition of territory in India; but great
and important have been the benefits resulting to
the State from our Indian possessions, in the increase of customs and excise, in the quantity of
treasure brought into the kingdom, and by our
being enabled to carry on the trade to China
without draining this kingdom of specie, which
it now could ill afford to part with, and by the

* Colonel Dow.

large

large fums paid at different periods to Government by the Eaft-India Company.

It feems, however, now to be allowed, that it would be carrying Quixotifm to too great a length, were we to abandon a country which we have fo nobly ftruggled to preferve; — and the next queftion naturally was, What would be the beft mode of government for India?

* The plan of the late Miniftry was, to fix a ftrong Government at home, to be conftantly under the eye of Parliament, poffeffing complete power both at home and abroad, to make all appointments, and to be looked up to in India as *the Government*.

There is a very curious paffage in the Ninth Report, which, I confefs, furprized me exceedingly when I read it firft: "that a fenior " merchant in Bengal was not a fervant of the " Supreme Council, as Mr. Haftings hazards " to call him, but their fellow fervant." — Men, who could for a moment entertain an opinion fo abfurd, may well be fuppofed capable

---

* Their plan was to eftablifh a board, to confift of feven Perfons, who fhould be invefted *with full power to appoint and difplace officers in India, and under whofe controul the whole Government of that country fhould be placed.*

Mr. Fox's fpeech, 18th November, 1783.—Debrett's Debates, vol. XII. page 43.

of joining in a plan for fixing the government of India, in Parliament-ſtreet Weſtminſter; but ſuch a Government could not poſſibly have laſted ſix months: deſtroy the energy and the vigour of *the Government in India*, and you will ſoon loſe the country. The rejected plan was admirably adapted for ſuch a purpoſe. The whole of the reaſoning in ſupport of this meaſure was ſo fallacious, that men muſt now wonder how it could have been attended to;—In truth, the old and wiſe ſyſtem of the Company, (under which the Duke of Richmond well obſerved, they flouriſhed to ſo great a degree) would never have been trenched upon, but from a miſchievous attempt to extend the power of patronage at home. Mr. Pitt has had good ſenſe enough to ſee this, and virtue enough to provide a remedy for the growing evil. In the time of Lord Clive, of Mr. Verelſt, and Mr. Cartier, and for the firſt thirty months of Mr. Haſtings's government, there never exiſted an idea in Leadenhall-ſtreet of appointing gentlemen abroad to ſpecific poſts*. Thoſe upon the ſpot are the proper judges of merit, and the only way to make

---

* A ſecretary, accountant, and mint-maſter, were appointed from hence to Bengal in former years, and their appointments occaſioned much diſcontent in India.

a Go-

a Government refpected and obeyed, is to have
in its poffeffion the power of reward and punifhment. The Directors referved to themfelves
the privilege of appointing civil fervants to their
fettlements, but they wifely left it to the Go-
vernors and their Council, to employ them.
When the regulating bill paffed in 1773, and
the Minifter began to tafte the fweets of Indian
patronage, the good old rules of the fervice
were broken down. Then it was that party,
cabal, and intrigue, were felt in every depart-
ment of the fervice, both at home and abroad.
Then it was that the Governor General of India was forced into a perfonal conteft with two
junior fervants; and now Mr. Haftings is accufed of temerity, for hazarding to call a fenior
merchant a fervant of the Supreme Council,
inftead of their fellow-fervant.

To complete this fyftem of abfurdity, it
was propofed, on the 18th of November, to
fix the government of India here. The gentlemen abroad would then indeed have been
fellow-fervants, but how there could have been
vigour in the government, how there could
have been obedience to orders, how the army
could have been commanded, how the revenues collected, how a dominion preferved, even

M 2   for

for fix months, I cannot comprehend. The Minifter of this country, while we could keep India, would have enjoyed a degree of power and pre-eminence hitherto unknown; fince the whole patronage of the Eaft, as well as an extenfive patronage at home, would have been vefted in his commiffioners.—The defeft of this fyftem is now fully feen, and was never more forcibly expofed than by Lord Stormont, who voted againft the former bill, in a. fpeech upon Mr. Pitt's bill. — His Lordfhip obferved, that the way to preferve and to govern India was to have a ftrong government eftablifhed in that country, under the control of a ftronger Government here. — By no other fyftem can India be preferved — But was that the fyftem of the compiler of the Ninth Report, or the fyftem which the late Minifters meant to eftablifh? Can they mean to fix a ftrong government in India, who call a junior merchant the fellow fervant of the Governor General of India, and accufe the latter of pre-fumption for endeavouring to fupport the dig-nity of his ftation? The government of India muft be in India, and the fervants of the Com-pany abroad muft look up to the governments

upon

upon the fpot — But on the other hand, every deviation from orders, every act of oppreſion or injuſtice, muſt be feverely puniſhed; for in proportion as the powers delegated to t'e governments are ſtrong, and ſtrong they muſt of neceſſity be, in proportion muſt be their reſponſibility — But the fpirit of defpotiſm at home, and equality abroad which the India bill of the late Miniſtry meant to eſtabliſh, was calculated to overthrow the Conſtitution of this country, and to deprive us of all we puſſeſs in Aſia.

If any thing had been wanting to eſtabliſh complete anarchy in Bengal, the bill for the better government of the territorial poſſeſſions and dependencies was admirably calculated to effect it — By one clauſe, the Company would have been deprived of a revenue of 600,000l. a year, collected now without oppreſſion or injuſtice — By other clauſes, innumerable landholders would have been difpoſſeſſed or fubject to vexatious conteſts, and by another clauſe, Engliſhmen who have ferved their country with honour to themfelves, and advantage to the State, were to be deprived of their franchiſe, and not permitted to fit for a

certain

ertain period in the Houfe of Commons. —
Perhaps this claufe was introduced to prevent
Mr. Haftings from contaminating a late virtu-
ous affembly on his arrival in England.

The claufe of Mr. Pitt's bill which obliges
every man ferving in India to declare the
amount of his fortune has been deemed a
harfh one. It is a facrifice to the delufion of
the moment, I prefume, but if it were extended
to contractors, commiffaries, dealers in loans,
and men of various defcriptions here, who have
grown rich from the public purfe, during the
late calamitous war, I fancy the world would be
convinced that more money may be acquired
in England in a week, than in India in twenty
years. — Harfh, however, as this claufe may be
deemed, it is mild indeed, compared to that in
a rejected bill, which precluded an Englifhman
from the honour of ferving his country in
Parliament, and from the privilege of defending
himfelf againft the efforts of ignorance and
malice, which I have often feen combined to
calumniate men of irreproachable characters.

Many infinuations have been thrown out, as if
Mr. Haftings depended upon the fupport of
the prefent Minifters, or of thofe poffeffed of

ftill

ftill greater power than the miniftere. Thefe
are infinuations only, and are totally unfounded.
Mr. Haftings's fupport was from the public at
large. — There has, indeed, been fome difference in the conduct of the late and the prefent Minifters. From what has already paffed,
I prefume Mr. Haftings will not now be condemned unheard, as he would have been laft
winter,—but the prefent minifters are refponfible
to the nation, for the good government of India; and if there is any thing in the character,
or the conduct of Mr. Haftings which renders
him unfit for his ftation, they are bound to recal him, and to punifh him. Mr. Haftings
has never fhrunk from refponfibility; he has
never attempted, by the low arts of cabal and
intrigue, to preferve his fituation, nor has he
defcended to the meannefs of deprecating the
vengeance of thofe who were inclined, laft
winter, to exert their power to the utmoft, in
order to crufh him.

Determined as his Majefty's Minifters were,
in 1782, to remove Mr. Haftings, what could
have faved him but the high opinion in which
his conftituents held him? Did they act ille-
gally or abfurdly, in differing in opinion from a
majority

majority of forty-three members of the Houfe Commons? Will any man of common fenfe believe, that if at that period, or fince, any one, even the moft minute of the charges brought againft Mr. Haftings, could have been fubftantiated, a bill for his removal would not have been carried without a diffenting voice? In the rejected bill, was there a claufe for Mr. Haftings's removal? Though his fuppofed mifconduct was ftated to have produced the neceffity for fo ftrong a meafure as that confeffedly was, yet the bill actually left Mr. Haftings the Governor General of Bengal, until the feven mighty monarchs fhould determine his fate in clofe divan'; for we have fince been given to underftand, *(credat Judæus!)* that it was uncertain whether Mr. Haftings was to be removed or not.

If any thing were wanting to expofe the fallacious bafis on which the rejected bill was founded, we have ample proof of it in the late advices from India, by which we know that peace and tranquility are reftored to every part of it; and to fecure us in the poffeffion of that great arm of the empire, we only wanted what I think Mr. Pitt's bill has fully eftablifhed, a

govern-

government, and a ftrong government in India, under the control of a ftill ftronger government at home.

In the courfe of our ftruggles, we have feen the power of the Government of this country unjuftifiably exerted to remove Mr. Haftings; and, unfupported by family connections, or Parliamentary intereft, but by the mere force of perfonal character, he has obtained a complete triumph over his opponents. Neither bribery nor corruption were reforted to, in fupport of him; and however a certain fet of gentlemen may attempt to miflead the public by afferting again, and again, that the proprietors are the fervants, of the fervants in India, and that the whole body is corrupt; yet every man of fenfe and obfervation muft treat thefe remarks as childifh and abfurd. The Proprietors have in fact preferved India to Great Britain, as Mr. Dempfter has often declared, who, at the minute the late Miniftry condemned the conduct of the Proprietors, and were themfelves determined to remove the Governor General, publicly defended them in the Houfe of Commons; and afferted, that he could conceive no act fo completely abfurd as the removal of

N   Mr.

Mr. Haftings, during the war would be, unlefs General Eliott had been fuperfeded in his command at the moment the Spanifh batteries were playing againft Gibraltar.

THE END.

BOOKS printed for J. DEBRETT, oppofite BURLINGTON HOUSE, PICCADILLY.

PARLIAMENTARY REGISTER.

This Day was Publifhed, Price 1s.

THE PARLIAMENTARY REGISTER, No. II. of the Prefent Parliament, containing an accurate, full, and impartial Account of all the Debates of the laft Seffion, collated with the Notes and Papers of feveral Gentlemen, who have very obligingly communicated the fame.

☞ At the defire of feveral Perfons of diftinguifhed Abilities and Rank, this Work was undertaken. The favourable Reception it has met with during the whole of the two laft Parliaments, not only demands the moft grateful Acknowledgements of the Editors, but encourages them to a Continuation of the fame through the prefent Parliament. For this Purpofe, and to prevent Mifreprefentation, they beg leave again to folicit the Affiftance of their former Friends, and every other Gentleman. A ftrict Attention will be paid to their Commands and Favours; nor will any Affiduity or Care be wanting to preferve that Truth and Accuracy, for which this Work has hitherto been diftinguifhed.

The PARLIAMENTARY REGISTER of the laft Parliament complete, viz. from 1780 to 1784, in fourteen Volumes. Price 5l. 8s. half-bound and lettered.

The PARLIAMENTARY REGISTER of the former Parliament, viz. from 1774 to 1780, in feventeen Volumes, Price 6l. 6s. half bound and lettered.

The REMEMBRANCER; or IMPARTIAL REPOSITORY of PUBLIC EVENTS. The AMERICAN WAR gave rife to this Work in 1775. Every authentic Paper relative to that War, as alfo with France and Spain, whether publifhed in ENGLAND or AMERICA, by the BRITISH MINISTRY, or the AMERICAN CONGRESS, are all carefully inferted in this Work. The Letters of the feveral Commanding Officers, Addreffes, Refolutions of the various Committees, Conventions, &c. To thefe have been prefixed, at the Defire of many Perfons, a Collection of authentic Papers refpecting the Difpute with America before the Commencement of Hoftilities. As the Remembrancer gave the beft and only Accounts of the Tranfactions of the War, the principal Encouragers of the Work wifhed to fee preferved and printed, in the fame Size, all thofe authentic Papers on the various Subjects of Difpute, from the Refolutions which gave rife to the Stamp Act in 1764, to the Battle of Lexington in 1775. This Volume accompanies the Remembrancer, and is called Prior Documents, or a Collection of interefting, authentic Papers, relative to the Difpute between Great Britain and America; fhewing the Caufes and Progrefs of that Mifunderftanding, from 1764 to 1775. Complete Sets of this valuable and interefting Work may be had of the Publifher in Seventeen Volumes. Price Six Guineas, half bound and lettered.

*** Thofe Gentlemen who are in want of any particular Numbers to complete their Sets, are earneftly intreated to order them as fpeedily as poffible.

The NEW FOUNDLING HOSPITAL FOR WIT: Being a Collection of fugitive Pieces in Profe and Verfe, not in any other Collection. A new Edition, confiderably improved and enlarged; in which are inferted feveral curious Pieces, by Lady Craven, the Marquis of Carmarthen, the Earls of Carlifle, Buchan; Nugent; the Lords Palmerfton, Mulgrave, Holland; Sir J. Moore, Right Hon. C. J. Fox, Right Hon. R. Fitzpatrick, Sir W. Jones, Dr. B. Franklin, J. Wilkes, D. Garrick, R. B. Sheridan, Sir Charles Hanbury Williams,

Williams, Mr. Gray, Mr. Mason, G. Ellis, R. Cumberland, B. Edwards, Capt. E. Thompson, &c. &c. which were not in the former Edition; together with several Pieces, now first printed from the Authors' Manuscripts. The Whole carefully revised, arranged, and corrected, in six Volumes. Price 18s. sewed.

The NEW PEERAGE; or, the Ancient and Present State of the Nobility of ENGLAND, SCOTLAND, and IRELAND; containing a genealogical Account of the Peers, whether by Summons or Creation; their Descents and collateral Branches; their Births, Marriages, and Issue; together with their paternal Coats of Arms, Crests, Supporters, and Mottoes, engraved. To which is added, The Extinct Peerage, comprehending an authentic Account of the Peers who have ever existed from the earliest Times. A new Edition. In three Volumes Octavo. Price 15s. in Boards.

*** The Editors profess to have given in these Volumes the clearest, most authentic, and the best digested Account of the noble Families of ENGLAND, SCOTLAND, and IRELAND, hitherto published; and, by omitting unnecessary Digressions, and ostentatious Quotations from Histories and biographical Memoirs, which only serve to increase the Price, have exhibited their Genealogies clear and explicit, so that every collateral Branch is seen with great Facility and Exactness, and few even of the Gentry of England, Scotland, and Ireland, who have intermarried with the Nobility of those Kingdoms, but may here discover by what Degree of Consanguinity they are allied.

A New Edition of COLLINS's PEERAGE of ENGLAND. In eight Volumes. Enriched with many valuable Additions, and continued to the present Time; with all the Arms finely engraved. Price 2l. 12s. 6d.

OBSERVATIONS on the COMMERCE of the AMERICAN STATES; by JOHN LORD SHEFFIELD. A new Edition, being the Sixth, much enlarged; with an Appendix, containing Tables of the Imports and Exports of Great Britain to and from all Parts; also the Exports of America, &c, with Remarks on those Tables, and on the late Proclamations, &c. With a copious Index. Price Six Shillings in Boards.

BIOGRAPHIA BRITANNICA; or, the Lives of the most eminent Persons who have flourished in Great Britain and Ireland, from the earliest Ages to the present Times. Collected from the best Authorities, printed and manuscript, and digested in the Manner of Mr. Bayle's Historical and Critical Dictionary. The second Edition, with Corrections, Enlargements, and the Addition of new Lives. By Andrew Kippis, D. D. F. R. S. and S. A. With the Assistance of the Rev. Joseph Towers, LL. D. and other Gentlemen. Volume the Third. Price 1l. 11s. 6d. in Sheets.

Of whom may be had the first and second Volumes of the above Work, Price 1l. 11s 6d. each, in Sheets.

*** The fourth Volume is in the Press, and will be published with all possible Expedition.

BIOGRAPHIA DRAMATICA, an historical and critical Account of the Lives and Writings of British and Irish Dramatic Writers, from the earliest Times to 1784; with Anecdotes and Remarks on every anonymous dramatic Performance. In two large Volumes octavo. Price 12s. in Boards.

OLD BALLADS, historical and narrative, with some of modern Date; now first collected and re-printed from rare Copies and Manuscripts, none of which are inserted in Dr. Percy's Collection; to which this Work may be considered as a proper Supplement. The second Edition; elegantly printed, in four Volumes octavo. Price 14s. sewed.

www.ingramcontent.com/pod-product-compliance
Lightning Source LLC
Chambersburg PA
CBHW020035030726
47499CB00007B/2441